To
FRANK
TESTANI

THANX FOR
COMING TO
THE SHOW —

10 20 93

CUSTOMERIZATION

CUSTOMERIZATION

by Murray Raphel

The **180 Rules** to increase your business by using radio, TV, newspaper, direct mail, telemarketing, promotions . . . *and more!*

Raphel Publishing
Atlantic City, New Jersey

CUSTOMERIZATION

Copyright © 1993 by Raphel Publishing

Cover Design by: Merlin Creative Graphics

Manufactured in the United States of America

ISBN 0-9624808-5-1

To Neil.

*I always thought I'd only have one partner in
my lifetime.
But the original, Ruth, gave me another.*

ACKNOWLEDGMENTS

This book is an across-the-board reference for small businesses for almost all forms of marketing, advertising and promotion. The ideas originally came from my forty years in business.

But when I needed specific information on specific subjects, I went to experts in each field, showed them what I had written and asked, "Does this make sense? Is it accurate? Do you agree?"

Each was kind enough to take their time to review what was written in their special field of expertise and write, call or fax me back with suggestions, additions, ideas, corrections.

So let me take a moment to acknowledge their help and assistance:

Radio: Radio Advertising Bureau, Kay Wallace and Larry Levis;

TV: TV Bureau of Advertising;

Newspaper: Newspaper Advertising Association;

Direct Mail: James Rosenfield;

Telephone Marketing: George Walther;

Speaking: Ty Boyd and Bill Gove.

Others who took the time to review portions of the book and offer kind words or gentle criticism include Kathleen Hughes who made sure every "t" was crossed, every "i" dotted and asked probing questions to make sure what I wrote made sense. Thanks also to Ray Considine, my first mentor in speaking and Ken Erdman, who co-authored *"The Do*

It Yourself Direct Mail Handbook," for their excellent objective and succinct criticism.

Most of all, I want to thank my two partners: wife Ruth and son Neil. They read the daily writings, were quick to praise, and even quicker to criticize and put what I was writing into proper perspective.

This book could not have been written without their help.

Murray Raphel
1993

FOREWORD

Finishing a lecture series the night before in Hattiesburg, Mississippi, I stepped out into a bright, sunny morning with my colleague, Eddie Nicholson, awaiting our pickup for the airport. With a few minutes to spare, I looked up and down the main street of a city that had been so cordial over the last week. I said, "Eddie, look down the street. There is at least one retailer that will do business. In fact, he may even be one of my Phoenicians." Eddie looked up and down both sides of the street. He even looked at the names, since I had mentioned my family background, to see if that would be a give-away, but saw no indication why one merchant would be more successful than the others.

Laughingly, I said, "Eddie, see that man standing out in front of that attractive jewelry store? His competition are all in the back of their stores hoping business will come in. After all, they have filled the stores with merchandise, they have advertised. Now they are waiting for the public to respond, but not the man in front of that jewelry store. He's out on the street. He's going to greet people walking by, and he will make sure that they come in to his store for he'll accompany them. He will be making sales while others are waiting."

As I read a pre-published copy of Murray Raphel's new book, it brought back that story. That book will, in Murray's typical pragmatic manner, tell each of us how to be out in front bringing the customer into the store.

What a name . . . "Customerization." A buzz word in recent years has been "niche marketing," but that is quite often misunderstood, for it seems to suggest that your success is dependent upon finding a particular product that others don't have or applying all of your resources to a narrowly defined group. Some can do this and succeed, but it certainly limits the opportunity. Murray, in turn, is teaching us that whatever the range of products we have, or how totally cosmopolitan is our customer base, we can, through "customerization," reach the masses by making them feel that we are committed to their individual needs.

As you read the book, you will sense what I know, and that is, the writer has been in your shoes. When I reflect upon the growth of IGA (in a competitive, and for some years a recessed market, we have, from 1989-1992, had 36 consecutive months of adding a new supermarket every 30 hours) I find the fingerprints of Murray on much that we do. From his own achievements in Atlantic City, he encouraged our overall thrust of "Hometown Proud." Doug Ivester, the President of Coca-Cola North America, keeps reminding me that this slogan has been a singular advantage in these challenging times.

When I want a shot of adrenaline . . . when my spirits are drooping just a bit . . . when I want to get on "top of the game," I simply dial Murray Raphel's number and receive a bit of his personal mentoring. Now I wish I could give to each of you that rare privilege. Perhaps you can't do it that way, but this book will be like a series of visits with Murray. Don't read it too rapidly . . . but if you do, know that you're going to go back, page by page, marking up the sides, dreaming and visualizing what his suggestions can mean to your business, and then exciting your associates, whether it be in marketing, advertising, promotion or the integration of all three.

  In your behalf, I thank Murray Raphel for writing this book for the benefit of all of us.

> Tom Haggai
> Chairman & CEO
> Independent Grocer's Alliance (IGA)

Contents

INTRODUCTION

Once upon a time. . .

Starting a business had set rules to follow. It went something like this:

1. You decided the business you wanted.
2. You put together some kind of business plan.
3. You borrowed the money from friends, relatives or the local bank.
4. You bought merchandise and opened the door.
5. You waited for the customer to come and buy what you had to sell.

Today . . .

You can still decide the business you want to have and you still need money to open the doors. But waiting for the customer to come to buy what you decide to sell is no longer good enough.

You no longer sell your wares to everyone. You sell to *someone.*

The more personalized the offer, the better the results. The sellers of goods identify their customers on a one-on-one basis. They know what their customers want to buy . . . and give it to them.

This process can be summarized in a new word: *Customerization.*

Customerization **works.**

Stan Golomb in Chicago puts together a program for dry cleaners offering turn-key customerization. He mails monthly cards with different specials to the stores' customers by name. More than 400 individual dry cleaners participate and are doing business because they make a specific offer to a specific customer.

Judd Goldfeder in Escondido, California has a similar program for restaurants. About 20 percent of his customers come in because of a simple postcard addressed to them by name.

Orville Roth has supermarkets in Oregon. He sends a simple fold-over mailer to his customers with monthly specials. He started by using a sweepstakes promotion to gather the names and addresses of current customers. His first promotion to this list had a 70 percent response. His return is still about 15 percent or more each month (a terrific return for a direct mail promotion) because . . . he writes to a specific customer offering them a specific value.

Leo Kahn, a 73-year-old entrepreneur, opened Fresh Fields, a health food style supermarket in the suburbs of Washington, D.C. a few years ago. When other supermarkets in his area were losing market share to growing wholesale clubs, he opened four new stores in less than three years!

What he discovered: there are people out there who want to buy healthy food. And all those folks have a common educational, financial and demographic background. He analyzed population groups across the U.S. who had the same demographics as his winners in Washington and is now opening in those locations. Why? Because he discovered what HIS SPECIFIC customers want . . . and he gives it to them.

Reward is an integral part of *Customerization.*

It is no longer enough to give the customer fair value for a fair price. People EXPECT to be rewarded and thanked over above and beyond the words after they make the purchase.

When we ran a Gold Card program for our retail clothing business, we offered it to 500 customers out of the thousands who shopped with us. But these 500 were responsible for more than 75 percent of our total business! Every month we wrote and offered them some "reward" for coming to the store. Our return averaged between 20 and 30 percent. (Compared to our mailings to everyone on our mailing list that averaged a 5% return.)

Why does this work?

"A (reward) increases the value you offer your customers with no or low cost to yourself as a partner." — William Ross, Professor of Marketing, University of Pennsylvania.

"You build long term relationships." — Tim Smith, American Airlines

"(You) build brand loyalty and incremental business." — Ray Noble, public relations manager, Avis

General Motors offers you a Visa card with an extra special reward: Every time you use the card you "earn 5 percent on every purchase" toward your next GM car or truck. They limit you to $500 a year for a maximum of $3,500 over 7 years. But what a reward

15

for using a credit card you would use . . . anyway!
Ford obviously thought so because they began an
almost identical program a few months later.

Another way to reward: Promotion Partners

The supplier can no longer indulge himself with the
luxury of image advertising in leading publications
and expect to sell merchandise. What do those ego
building ads mean to the independent businessman?
Very little.

No customer ever came to our clothing store with a
copy of a fashion ad in the *New York Times Sunday
Magazine* and asked, "Do you have this
merchandise?"

"Traditional mass media advertising doesn't work
for the small store," says Donna Hanberry, Executive
Director of the Alliance of Independent Store Owners
and Professionals. "TV, radio and most daily papers
reach a large geographic area. For the local drugstore,
dry cleaner, grocer or clothing retailer, it doesn't make
sense when most of your potential customers live
three miles from your store."

It's time to let your supplier know (in case they
missed it) that in the past few years there was a
revolution in how advertising dollars are being spent.

Listen to this quote from Rick Fitzdale, chairman of
the advertising agency Leo Burnett: "While national
advertising isn't devalued, the war is really won at
retail."

The suppliers HAVE to help you sell your product if
THEY want to be in business tomorrow morning.

Some enlightened suppliers have seen the writing
on the wall.

• **ConAgra's Country Pride** chicken divided its $115 million national advertising budget into budgets to be used by *individual* supermarkets or chains. Each retailer chooses how many ads and/or promotional events Country Pride will do in their markets, which products will be featured and which media will be used. Here's a quote from Dick Lynch, senior vice president, "Country Pride needed a program that can get consumers to the shelf and has the power to get the retailers to merchandise the product."

ConAgra knows their merchandise is sold at the point-of-sale and not from the four-color glossy ad in a consumer magazine.

• **Spector Photo in Brussels, Belgium** makes a computer program available for the 600 independent photographic shops they service. This computer program keeps all the data for each customer. When a customer brings film to the store, the owner punches up his or her name on the computer. The owner can see all the information on that customer: the film they buy and the prints they want. The computer then prints out a "reward" discount. After six purchases, the customer spends their accumulated discount (usually 10 percent) on any new purchases. Look at Spector's enlightened slogan for the retailers they service: "We don't sell you prints. We sell you profit." Says Johan Mussche, Spector's president, "We make our independent dealers into real business partners."

• **M & M Candy** changed their allocations of advertising dollars one Halloween and set aside one half of their total advertising budget for in-store advertising. Their volume increased!

• **Greenwich Workshop** is the largest distributor of signed limited edition prints of American artists. They supply quality catalogues and "sell sheets" to their more than 1,000 independent dealers. They prepared a "Direct Mail Handbook" for each dealer and ran seminars showing how direct mail would increase their business. It did.

• **Bijttegbier** is one of Belgium's largest wholesalers and importers of tableware. The company put together a marketing program for brides-to-be using newspaper, radio and TV. They signed up 21,000 couples (or one out of three brides-to-be in Belgium). The company prepared a mailing piece for their dealers. The dealers sent the mailer. The sales: $19 million or double the previous year's business!

The list goes on...because manufacturers realize:

Today's customer is far more difficult to reach with traditional mass media.

Today's customer is cynical about mass advertising messages.

Today's customer is busier. Harder to reach with mass media.

Today's customer is more ethnic. (Example: There are 25 million Latinos in the U.S., which is the same number as the total population of Canada.)

The following pages give you more information on *Customerization*: how it works in all the media available to you.

1

WHY YOU SHOULD USE *CUSTOMERIZATION* IN YOUR ADVERTISING

I once counted fifteen magazine ads set in reverse type. *(But everyone knows reverse ads are harder to read than black on white ads.)*

I listened to a radio commercial the other day for a men's clothing store and heard them advertise twelve different items with the regular price AND the sale price. *(Don't they know no one can remember all those prices?)*

I watched half a dozen TV ads one evening and never found out what they were selling. *(They were so busy being clever I never found out a reason I should buy the merchandise, whatever it was.)*

I receive, on average, twenty direct mail pieces a day. I throw most of them away with but a few seconds' glance. *(Don't they know there are ways to have me stop, look and read?)*

I mention all this because there are certain techniques that seem to work most of the time in different media. Through reading, watching, and most of all, doing, I have found out what detours to avoid and what roads to take.

I inwardly tremble when I hear the phrase "junk mail" describing my favorite advertising — direct mail. I once protested in a letter-to-the-editor, "True, there IS junk mail. But there is also junk TV advertising, junk radio adverting, junk newspaper advertising . . ."

Most advertising is boring, unattractive and doesn't do the basic job of having the customer buy what the business is trying to sell.

After hundreds (thousands?) of books on advertising and thousands (tens of thousands?) of surveys, the same errors occur time and time again in all forms of advertising.

The major error: most businesses advertise what they want to sell and not what their customers want to buy.

Once you start thinking in terms of the customer rather than yourself, you're on your way to doing more business.

I wrote the following pages on what I've learned about different forms of advertising.

Some of it is first hand knowledge from having done it.

Some of it is sending what I wrote to experts in the fields and asking, "Is this correct?"

Some of it is from trade associations, who, though understandably biased in their approach, still offered valuable pointers on the best way to use their medium.

Some of it is from reading and re-reading the dozens of advertising books in my library and finding out where the experts DO agree with one another.

Some of it is from reacting as a consumer as well as a businessman.

All of it is important for you to know before planning your next advertising campaign. The following pages include years of testing ideas with customers.

I've put together for you what I believe are rules that can work best for you and your business.

2

So, You Want To Write An Ad

Good. Here Are 60 Rules To Follow.
   20 for headlines
   20 for copy
   20 for illustrations.

Question: What makes a good newspaper ad?
Answer: One that makes the customer buy from you.

   FACT: Newspapers reach more than 113 million adults in the U.S. every day. About six out of ten say they read every page. Nine out of ten read the general news. And if your business is looking for a specific gender, remember 9 out of 10 men read the sports pages and 8 out of 10 women read the entertainment pages.
   Most newspaper readers are subscribers (7 out of 10) which means it's a guaranteed delivery into the home of your customers, unlike radio or TV that deliver to the home only when the viewer or listener decide to view or listen.
   It's a very important medium to consider for your

business since more ad dollars are spent in newspaper than any other medium — nearly $34 billion a year.

Newspapers eat up 25 percent of the ad dollars spent nationwide—but for local advertising, they use half the available ad dollars. (Next: TV and yellow pages with about 13 percent each.)

Here are some guidelines on headlines, copy and illustrations we learned through the years:

THE HEADLINE

The average person spends four seconds before turning the newspaper page. In those four seconds they look at the news headlines first. You better say something that makes them want to stop and read the headline of your ad. Something that makes them want to keep on reading.

The average woman only reads four ads in an average newspaper so put *news* into the headline. Something that is new, just-arrived, first-time, unique — those are key words that make the reader read.

1. Promise a benefit or provoke curiosity.
Remember there are only two things that people buy: Solutions to problems and good feelings. Think of those two criteria next time you sit down to write a headline for one of your products or services. Stress the benefit of your product, not the product itself. If the shoes you sell have crepe soles (feature) say they are "shock absorbing" (benefit). If the suits

you sell are a blend of dacron and wool (feature) say they can be worn "year round" (benefit). Advertisements with headlines that promise a benefit are read by four times more people than headlines that don't have benefits. Charles Mills, vice president of O.M. Scott, largest grower of lawn seed in the world, said, "People are interested in their lawns. Not in our seeds."

2. Put the name of the product in the headline if possible. Not the name of your business. Put your name someplace else in the ad. Not in the headline unless it has a special meaning "Only at (name of your business) will you find (name of item)." Most people like to see the name of their business at the top of the ad. Most customers could care less. The bottom of the ad is fine . . .

3. Long headlines pull as well (and often better) than short headlines. Headlines with more than ten words have much better readership than shorter headlines.

4. Don't be clever for the sake of being clever. A recent ad for automobiles promoted new cars with catalytic converters with this headline: "Are you allergic to cats?" If the reader was, they stopped reading after the first sentence because the ad had nothing to do with cats.

5. Have a 'big idea.' David Ogilvy said: "Unless your campaign is built around a big idea, it will pass like a ship in the night." You have to find out what's unique about the product you are advertising. The more yours-alone facts you put in your copy, the easier it is to sell your merchandise.

6. Sell one idea at a time. Otherwise you confuse the reader.

7. Make it "news"worthy. A "new" product. A "new" solution. Ads with news in the headlines pull about 20 percent better.

8. Use certain words in headlines because...they work. They include (but are not limited to) New, Free, How to, Amazing, Introducing, Guarantee, You, Now... If your ad is directed to a certain audience, put them in the headline (asthmatics, people with rheumatism.) One ad that worked: **"Sixty Days Ago They Called Me Baldy"** You can be sure bald-headed men read THAT ad.

9. Include a local reference if possible. Supermarkets that promote products grown in their state report a dramatic increase in sales. People want to be identified with indigenous merchandise. There's a pride in buying that-which-is-theirs. Which is one reason why Mondale won Minnesota and Dukakis won Massachusetts when almost every other state turned them down.

10. Don't be clever. Double entendre, puns, headlines written to grab your attention but have no follow

26

through simply don't work. A cable TV network ran a series of ads with prominent people making statements like, **"Murphy Brown Moves To 60 Minutes."** They began each of these ads with copy that said, "Well, that isn't true, but if it *were* true..." And most people stopped reading. We once wrote an ad for snowsuits we bought in Finland as follows:

"We Went To Hel-Sinki And Back To Bring You These Snowsuits." Funny. But didn't sell snowsuits. The following week we ran the same ad but changed the headline to:

"In Our Thirty Years In Business, We Never Sold So Much Of One Item In So Short A Time." That sold jackets. People read the headline and said, "I wonder what it is that sold so well.."

11. Put the headline under an illustration. Why? Because that's how people read. You'll pick up an extra percentage of readers because that's how they're used to seeing a news story. If your ads looks more like an editorial page, your readership will increase.

12. Don't write your headline in capital letters. Setting your ad in lower case INSTEAD OF SETTING IT LIKE THIS will increase readership. Here's why: we learn to read in lower case letters like this sentence. Yes, the headline will be set in a larger type face but still set it in lower case.

13. Make the headline easy to understand. John
Caples, an expert in headline writing and former VP
of BBD&O said, "People are thinking of other things
when they see your ad." Don't make them think.
Make them act.

14. Make it believable. I'll read **"How To Lose Ten
Pounds In Two Weeks."** I won't read **"How To
Lose Ten Pounds In 24 Hours"** One is believable.
One isn't.

15. Make it for your audience. You use a different
headline if your audience is a five year old child or a
sixty year old grandmother.

16. Tell a story. People like to read stories and your
headline will keep them reading into the body copy
if the story is interesting. Here's a headline we used
for men's terry robes:
**"We First Saw These In The Crillon Hotel On
The Place de la Concorde In Paris."**
We actually did. First time we saw thick, terry robes
hanging in a hotel room's closet. We came home
and ordered them for our store and this headline
sold the robes!

17. Solve a problem. We found we could monogram
a child's name on an inside tag or the front of a
special brand of children's raincoats. Most children's
raincoats are yellow and you can't tell one from
another in the cloakroom. Your child often comes
home with someone else's coat. Our headline read:

"Can't Lose This Raincoat 'Cause It Has Their Name On It." We sold out in three days!

18. **Fulfill a dream.** John Caples wrote this classic: "They laughed when I sat down at the piano"and it sold courses on learning to play the piano through mail courses.

19. **Offer excellent value.** After forty years of writing headlines, there are less than a dozen that work every time. Here's our favorite. It will work for your business by simply substituting the prices and the item:
  "Would You Buy A $30.00 Shirt on Sale For $14.99?"
  It tells original price, sale price and makes you want to read more to find out why.

20. **Last, but not least, don't forget to use a headline.** If you think that sounds unbelievable, look at the automobile and foods ads in your local newspaper. They either have no ad (just the name of the business up there at the top) or innocuous phrases like **"Mid Winter Clearance"** which means . . . nothing.
A final word: Try different headlines for the same product. John Caples said he tried different headlines for the exact same product and one would pull as much as 20 times more business than the others.
  Doubleday Books ran this headline successfully for years:

"Buy Any Of These Four Books For 99¢"
Until someone came up with the same offer — but a different headline that worked much better:
"Buy Three Books For 99¢ - Get One Free."

THE COPY

The body copy of your ad is read by only one out of ten readers. The trick is to catch them with the headline and keep them reading with the first few paragraphs. If you can have someone read the first 50 words of what you write, they will probably read the next 250 words.

It is impossible to underestimate the power of words. Or even a word. Some examples:

• How one word doubled the business of a hair shampoo. The instructions read, "Wet hair. Apply lather. Rinse thoroughly." And then a bright person added one word that doubled the business: "Repeat."

• World famous salesman Elmer Wheeler was known for using a phrase or two to increase sales. A drugstore chain wanted to increase their sales of milk shakes. At that time, some customers requested an egg in their milk shake which added to the cost (and profit). Wheeler's suggestion tripled sales: When the customer asked for a milkshake, the counter person would say, "One egg or two?" Almost everyone said "one" (The others said "two").

• Helena Rubinstein cosmetics couldn't understand why department stores were turning down the free give-away Rubinstein offered. We analyzed their presentation and came back with the answer:

"You are using two wrong words. The first one is when your headline says, "A gift from Helena Rubinstein." Wrong. It should be a gift from the store.

Second: You offer the customer "free coupons." It should be a "gift certificate." Supermarkets give coupons. You give gift certificates. Same product. Different word. By making these two simple changes, nearly every department store offered the free gifts.

• When you visit Disneyland or Disney World, employees know you are not a customer. You are a "guest." This simple word change is reflected in courtesy shown. We are nicer to "guests" than we are to "customers."

• I like the way our British cousins call Life Insurance companies Life ASSURANCE companies. I guess that means I'm paying money to "assure" I keep on living. U.S. companies tell me I win only if I die.

And so, when writing the copy for your ad, remember the importance words play.

And . . . Here Are Twenty Ways To Keep Them Reading:

21. Get to your main point . . . fast! Most teachers of copywriting will show how you can cut out the first three paragraphs and probably make the copy more saleable. Your beginning copy should expand on the benefit promised in the headline.

22. Make sentences short. Only 12 to 15 words. Make paragraphs short. Two or three sentences. This

31

gives you lots of "white space" around your copy. Makes it easier to read. Remember readers "scan" rather than "read."

23. Don't set copy wider than three inches. Here's why: the eye drops down to the next line after 3 to 4 inches. Especially at normal 8 point type size. (This is 12 point.)

24. Don't exaggerate. Make sure "the story isn't better than the store." Promise a lot and deliver more.

25. Be specific. The Five W's still work. To quote Kipling:
"I keep six honest serving men
(They taught me all I knew);
Their names are What and Why and When
And How and Where and Who."

26. Write as though you were talking to someone in your living room. Chatty, comfortable, easy-to-read and understand.

27. Set your copy in serif type. Not sans serif. Here's why: Sans serif is difficult to read. This copy is set in serif type. It has little "hooks" on the end of each letter which makes it easier for the eye to follow along.

28. Long copy sells as much as short copy. As long as it's interesting to read.

29. Write to the present tense. Positively, absolutely avoid the past perfect tense. The "has been" or "were done." Writing in the present tense means something is happening now. Writing in the past tense means it's over with, long gone, in the past. . . . who cares?

30. Use words people understand. I once wrote copy on a new song that I said "was the best music I've heard since Glenn Miller went down in the English channel." I showed the copy around the office and everyone younger than 30 asked me, "Who's Glenn Miller?"

31. Use testimonials. Of people who actually bought from you or used your product. Can be big stars. But your local customers are much less expensive to use and can be just as effective. ("Hey, here's a picture of Mary Simpson. I know Mary . . .")

32. Include the price. We once ran an ad for a little girl's sheepskin coat. The price was very high and our buyer advised us against telling the price in the ad. We persuaded her saying, "Why did you buy it if you didn't think you could sell it?" Nine out of ten newspaper readers said pricing influences their product selection and desire to buy. If you don't tell them, you haven't influenced them.

33. If it's on sale, tell me how much I'm saving. Food ads are most guilty of this. They yell "sale" at the top of their ads but don't tell me how-much-was-it. If it's on sale, great. But tell me two things: (1) the original price and (2) how much I'm saving.

34. Read the award winning ads and copy them. Why not? Go to the art museum and see the artists copying the masters. Most popular singers tell you they started by copying the style of someone they admired. That's how you start. Eventually your own style will develop.

35. Does your ad include all the pertinent information? Take a look at the copy in mail order catalogues. In a very small space they tell you what you want to know. Is it washable? What sizes does it come in? What colors? The more you tell, the more you sell.

36. The word "FREE" is still the most powerful word in the English language. "Buy two for $10, get one **free**" pulls 40 percent better than "Half Price" or "50 percent off."

37. Put a coupon in the ad and increase response. At least 10 percent more people will remember seeing your ad if you include a coupon. When Danielle Barr took over as head of advertising at National Westminster Bank in London, she came from a background of direct marketing. She called in the agencies responsible for the bank's advertising and told them she wanted a coupon in all future advertising. The agencies squirmed, were uncomfortable, mentioned "disturbing design layout" and "not the image of the bank" and "what's the reason." Danielle carefully explained that in the million plus readership in the London newspapers, someone, somewhere, somehow would respond to the coupons. And they were excellent prospects for area managers to follow up with because they now had the customer's name and address. (Yes, it worked.)

38. Put the coupon in the lower right hand corner. Here's why: It's easier to tear out.

39. Anticipate questions. What would you ask yourself about the offer you are making? That's what most folks are asking themselves while they're reading. Sooooo, answer their questions. That's one reason Question & Answer copy is so effective. Gives you a chance to anticipate the objections. . . and answer them.

40. Remember the rule of three: Say what you're going to say. Say it. Say what you said. Follow that outline and you're way ahead of most copywriters.

THE ILLUSTRATION

A headline and copy capture your attention and explain what you have to sell. If, however, you can add an illustration to your ad you will increase readership. Here are rules to follow to make sure they keep on reading after they see the illustration.

35

41. Show the product in use. Photos of people using your product enhance credibility

42. Put the illustration at the top of the ad with a caption underneath. And then the headline. And then the body copy. That's how people read.

43. Use photographs instead of illustrations. They attract greater readership and sell more merchandise. Exception: many newspapers have older presses and cannot reproduce good quality photographs. That was true with us and so we used illustrations. Also, certain fashion ads use illustrations to convey a certain "look." Good example: Lord and Taylor's ads in *The New York Times*.

44. Does the finished ad "look" like *your* business? Or *any* business? The reader should recognize the ad as your ad and not someone else's. In an advertising class we taught, we would place, in the front of the room, ads from five local supermarkets with the store names taken off. We gave the class a paper with the names of the supermarkets and told them to match the names on their papers with the ads displayed. No one ever did it correctly.

45. Does the picture alone tell the story? This rule also works in television. Here's how: turn off the sound. Just look at the pictures. Do you know what is being advertised? If you don't, it's not a good ad. Same for illustrations in a magazine. If I covered up the copy and your name, would I know what you're trying to sell?

46. Make the illustration ask, "What does this mean?" If the picture is provocative, the reader will continue reading to find out what it's all about.

47. Make the picture show what happens when your product is used. The clothes come out whiter in the washing machine if they buy your cleaner. The children win prizes in the Easter parade wearing your clothing. We once did an ad for the service department of an automobile agency with a photograph showing used parts in a plastic bag in the trunk of the car. The point: The firm REALLY did the work and really did put in new parts. And here are the old parts to prove it. Since so many people do not have confidence in auto repairs, this made them feel more "comfortable." And the service department's business increased because of this one illustration.

48. Use photographs of real people. Testimonials are very important. Good example: contests. Does anybody really win? Publisher's Clearing House shows their truck pulling up to winners' houses in their TV ads and videotaping the reaction when the person is told they just won a million dollars. That's effective!

49. Keep illustrations simple. One person in the ad. One product in the ad. Keep it uncluttered.

50. If possible: Use a baby, an animal or something sexy. Those are proven attention-grabbers.

51. Use color. More and more newspapers are offering good color reproduction. In the past few offered it and those that did often had poor registration (the color didn't fall where it should and a hat became part of the flesh color of the face and part the color of the hat.) Today, modern presses have much better quality control. Your cost is about 50 percent more than black and white. But the ad can pull as much as 100 percent more readership. Good value. Besides, who wants to look at black and white meat or black and white produce from the supermarket?

52. Use captions under your illustrations. They are read by twice as many people who will read the copy in your ad. So make them selling sentences!

53. Make the illustrations look like they are part of an editorial. You see more and more advertising done this way because...it attracts about 50 percent MORE readers.

54. Vertical ads pull better than horizontal ads. About 25 percent more. One reason: people fold the newspaper and since most of the editorial appears on the top part, they read that section and then...turn the page.

55. The bigger the ad, the greater the response.
But not as much as you think. Using a factor of 100 percent reading a full page ad, here are the percentages if reduced:

Half page ad:	74 percent
One third page ad:	62 percent
One quarter page ad:	68 percent

Carefully think whether the extra exposure is worth the dramatic extra cost.

56. Running an ad in reverse type (white on black) will not attract readers. Just the opposite. It turns them off. Too difficult to read, so let's turn the page. Most astonishing example was a recent ad from a motor club that advertised membership with a coupon printed in reverse. Unless you had a pen with white ink, it was impossible to fill out.

57. Sell the merchandise, not the design. Many graphic artists are concerned with winning awards for their great designs and you're concerned with filling the register. Remind them your goal is what pays their salary.

58. Be wary of type on color backgrounds. Using black type on a dark blue background might be aesthetically attractive but you can't read the copy! If you can't read the copy you can't sell the merchandise!

59. Re-check the basics. Do you have the name of your business in the ad? Do you have the address?

Do you have a phone number for me to call? Do
you have the name of someone I can talk to when I
call? If you have free parking, have you told me
where it is? Look at the ads in this morning's
newspaper. Few, if any, remember to put in all items
we just mentioned.

60. The Bottom Line: If an ad works, repeat it.

Why Newspaper Advertising Works:
• Believability
• Mass exposure
• Lots of room to write descriptions
• You can go back and read it again
• You can rip it out and save it
• Targeted sections (sports, social..)
• Can use coupons
• Can pick days to advertise

Why Newspaper Advertising Doesn't Work:
• Fewer people reading
• Rates climbing faster than circulation
• Your ad is one of many ads
• Average reader spends 4 *seconds* on a page
• Audience it does NOT reach well includes 18 -
  34 year olds, out of towners
• Coupon redemption declining
• Can't determine placement of your ad

3

Radio:
"And now, a few words from our sponsor..."

The customer was someone we had not seen before in our store. She bought several items. As they were being wrapped we asked the question we always addressed to new arrivals, "Where did you hear about our store?"

"Oh," she said, "I heard your radio commercial just the other day."

"Really," we said, and thanked her for shopping with us.

As she left we realized that the greatest strength of radio is that the commercials never die. In fact, they hardly fade away.

Because . . . *we had not advertised on radio for three months!* Yet she heard our commercial "just the other day."

Yes, it was part of a long running campaign. But the fact remained we had been off the air all that time . . . and the ad was still remembered.

Radio is a valuable marketing tool for your business.

It informs, educates, is flexible, targetable, and intrusive.

Radio's unique strength is that it triggers the imagination. It is far, far more powerful to "think" of an image you hear being described than seeing the actual image. Comedian Stan Freberg wrote the following copy for a radio commercial. Imagine you are listening to the radio and you hear . . .

"Okay people, now, when I give the cue, I want the 700 foot mountain of whipped cream to roll into Lake Michigan which has been drained and filled with hot chocolate. Then the Royal Canadian Air Force will fly overhead towing a ten-ton maraschino cherry which will be dropped into the whipped cream to the cheering of 25,000 extras . . ."

The mental imagery of those words is far more powerful than seeing it happen on a TV screen.

There were those who predicted radio's decline and fall when TV arrived. What-really-happened: TV became the mass messenger and radio became the niche marketeer. Your customers pick, choose and listen to the type of radio format they like. There are many and varied but the most listened-to are (in this order) country, adult contemporary, religious, oldies, Top 40, News/Talk, Standards, Spanish, Soft Rock, Urban/Black, Easy Listening, Classic Rock, Jazz and Classical. The top two make up over one third of all the radio stations (country: 16.6 percent, adult contemporary, 19.2 percent.)

What you're doing when **you** choose the station where you advertise: *customerizing* your message for your customer.

We found, through the years, in our retail business,

that radio worked very effectively when used in one
of two ways:

• **Institutional advertising.** Who we are, what we
do and why you should come and shop with us. And
the ad runs for weeks and months.

• **Saturation advertising.** When you can "own" a
radio station with a flurry of radio commercials just
before the big sale in your store. You buy a month's
worth of commercials and use them up in one to three
days. They run every hour of the day because
somewhere, sometime, someone is listening to radio.

It figures. Nearly every single person in the U.S. has
at least one radio (99 percent by the last census). And
if the radio is not turned on at home, it can turn you
on at work (where 6 out of 10 people listen) or in the
car (where 9 out of 10 listen).

With more than 9,300 commercial radio stations on
the air (almost evenly divided between AM and FM)
and 600 million radios in use—somebody's listening,
somewhere, sometime.

The average American listens to radio more than 3
hours every day! Your goal is to figure out who's
listening where. And when.

More and more businesses are spending more and
more money on radio. Revenues are over $9 billion
and increasing yearly. In all businesses from autos to
computers to banks to supermarkets, to furniture and
drug products —all are spending more and more
money every year on radio. The more you know
about what works and what doesn't, the more
successful your ad will be.

Here's the cutting edge of present radio advertising:

integrated marketing. Many radio stations are building a data base of their listeners from contests and call-ins. They can then approach you with this offer: "When you buy advertising from us, we will send a direct mail piece from your business with a special offer for our listeners only . . ."

Radio represents a small percentage of total advertising in the U.S. — only about 6 percent of all ad dollars. But it can be very effective if you know the answers to the most-asked questions. So let's play the 20 Questions Game.

This time . . . about radio.

THE 20 RULES FOR RADIO ADVERTISING

61. Hasn't radio reached its saturation point? Is anybody still buying a radio?
A: They're buying and buying and buying and . . . Nearly 600 million radios are in use in the U.S. That's up from 456 million in 1980.

62. What radio station should I use?
A: The one your customers listen to. That's not difficult to find out. Ask. We sent questionnaires to our customers every year asking about different services the store offered, what media they read, listened to or watched. In our area there are 12 radio stations. We did most of our advertising on the station we liked. After all, if we liked it , our customers would like it, right? Wrong. When the surveys came back we discovered 67% of our

customers were listening to one station. *But it wasn't the station we were listening to!*
We switched our advertising dollars to this one station. Because . . . it is a proven fact that your customer of tomorrow is listening to the same station as your customer of today. They have the same demographics (age, income, number of children), geographics (live in the same area) and psychographics (have cars, hobbies, participate in similar sports).

63. When should I advertise?

A: Most people tend to listen to the news. We always tried to buy "adjacencies" to the news broadcasts. Yes, it costs more but if more people are listening, it's worth more.

64. How many commercials does a radio station have an hour?

A: If you guessed 20 or 30 you're wrong. It just seems that way. On the AM stations — which have MORE commercials than FM, there is an average of 11.6 commercial minutes an hour.

65. How loyal are radio listeners?

A: Lot more loyal than TV. "This listener loyalty factor is a big plus for radio. It represents a major difference between TV and radio today," says James Garrity, Director of Advertising, IBM. Echoes Marcos Rada, public affairs manager of American Express Travel Related Services, "We choose radio because it is more flexible and more targeted to pinpoint the specific customers we want by using certain stations. Radio is more effective than TV or newspaper."

66. What products are advertised most on radio?

A: In terms of national advertising, food products are number one, then cars, then financial services, then travel, then beer, ale, wine, then retail stores. Those categories provide nearly 60 percent of radio's advertising dollars.

So if you're in there somewhere, you should consider radio because those folks have figured out it works for them. (Businesses that use radio least: sporting goods, toys, jewelry, photo shops).

67. What time of the year do people listen most to the radio?

A: Seems constant. In the top 25 markets, the difference between the highest listenership (winter) and lowest (summer) is only a few percentage points.

68. Is there one big, terrific advantage over other media?

A: Yes. Speed. If pushed (and you have a cooperative radio station) you can put a message on radio in a few hours. Or less. It simply takes a much longer time to prepare a newspaper ad. A much, much longer time to prepare a direct mail piece. And much, much, much longer time to put together a TV commercial.

46

69. Is it expensive?

A: Yes, but . . . there always seems to be a "deal" in radio. Buy X amount of spots in the best time spot and they will often throw in "extras" in the wee hours of the morning. You can often barter more easily with radio than with any other advertising medium. ("If you give us ten $25 gift certificates from your business, we'll give you $250 worth of radio advertising if you also buy X amount of regular advertising.")

70. Every station that comes into my business tells me they're number one in the ratings and show me their Neilsen or Arbitron charts to prove it. How can they *all* be number one.?"

A. Believe it or not, they can be—but in different time sequences and different age brackets. One station might be number one in listenership in early morning drive time. They have a well-known announcer who turns everybody on (or whom everybody turns on). Another station is number one for the adult population ages 34 to 50. Another station is number one for late night programming. Another station...well, you get the idea. The rating services rate different age groups, different time slots. It's difficult for a station NOT to be number one. . .somewhere, sometime. Your job: Select the Number One for the audience you want to reach for your business. Ask to see the actual ratings and find out how the station's rating fits into your potential audience.

AND THEN: ask who else is advertising on the

station. Then call them and ask if they are satisfied. Non-competitive businesses will share this information with you.

71. Is there a technique for writing a radio script that works most of the time?

A: David Ogilvy offers one simple technique in his book "Ogilvy on Advertising." We've tested it many times and it consistently works for us. Here it is:
1. Identify your brand (the name of your business) early in the commercial.
2. Identify it often (mention your firm's name again and again and again and..)
3. Promise the listener a benefit early in the commercial.
4. Repeat the benefit (again and again and again and again and again and...)

If you memorize those four points, you are way ahead of most radio commercials who ignore those four very basic principles.

72. How often should I change my commercial?

A: Not as often as you think. There is an old advertising story about the owner of a major corporation who asked his agency how many people were working on his account.

"Fifty one," said the head of the agency. "Fifty one?" said the surprised owner. "What do they all do?"

The agency owner replied, "Well, one of them is working on some new ideas and the other 50 are out there convincing your people NOT to change the ad that's working so well now."

You will become tired, bored and anxious with your present radio ad much more quickly than the listener, many of whom will hear it the first time the next time it runs.

One reason why it pays to repeat: many people will simply not hear the commercial because they are working or preoccupied with some other activity.

73. If you could give me one way to make my commercial more listened-to, what would it be?

A: A sound. Something that's "different" and will make people listen. A travel agency did a memorable ad by starting their commercial with the sound of a cruise ship's foghorn. Or an expression ("We make money the old fashioned way. We earn it.")

One sound to seriously consider is . . . silence. A very, very powerful tool on radio. So powerful it can sometimes backfire. One example was a supermarket that wanted to prove to listeners their stores' prices were lower than anyone else. Here was the commercial:

Good morning ladies and gentlemen. At this time,
Fred's Foodland would like to list for you the
names of all the other stores in the area that are
presently selling food for less than Fred's Foodland.
So grab a pencil and paper and we'll list them for
you in alphabetical order. Ready? Here they are...

Which was followed by 20 seconds of silence and then the concluding message:

*"The previous message was brought to you as a
public service by Fred's Foodland."*

Great commercial. Except that listeners called the
station to find out why they had gone off the air.
The station promptly canceled the commercial.

74. How much product can I sell in one ad?
A: One. Imagine a furniture store listing fifteen
items with the original price and the sale price in a
one minute commercial. The audience will
remember . . . nothing! Sell a storewide sale. Sell a
newly-arrived product. Sell a specific brand.
That's it.

75. How about music in my radio commercial.
A: Good. If it works. Bad if it doesn't.

Be wary of jingles. The good ones are very
expensive. Local amateur jingles sound . . . amateur.
Another problem with jingles (including the
professional ones) is you can't understand many of
the words. People don't concentrate on listening to
the radio—they just listen to the radio. I like David
Ogilvy's line on singing commercials: Would you go
into a store and expect the sales person to start
singing at you?

76. Should I use well known radio personalities?
A: Sure. You might have to pay an extra "talent fee"
but the cost is worthwhile because the audience
identifies with the individual. We would give well
known radio personalities a very sketchy outline of
what we wanted to sell. Often just the product and

the price and tell them to say whatever they wanted to say. The commercials were far, far better because the audience knew they were off-the-cuff, extemporaneous and sounded well, more "believable."

77. Who writes the script?

A: The radio station has full time people who do just that — they write what you want to sell. And yes, in smaller stations it can be the salesperson who sold you the time. Insist that the salesperson bring the finished script for you to review and the finished cassette of the ad BEFORE it goes on the air.

Bring in some other folks in your business to listen to the finished advertisement. (You might be caught up in the euphoria of hearing the name of your business and therefore believe WHATEVER is said must be great because it's *you*). Your salesmen will make any corrections for you.

78. Should I alternate the times when my ad runs?

A: Yes. Running your ad different times on different days makes the customer feel they hear the ad many more times than it actually runs. There are exceptions. If a certain time slot works for you (like the news adjacencies we talked about) then keep on using it. Another good example is if a special time ties in with a special characteristic of your business. One advertiser became well known because his ad was broadcast every day at the same time because . . . well, let's listen:

"Good morning. It's 9:13. And today's news is

*brought to you by the Boardwalk National Bank at
913 Atlantic Avenue..."*
That worked.

79. Should I use my own voice?
A: Only if it's very distinctive or if your voice has a
professional sound. That should eliminate most
people reading this sentence. But a distinctive voice
can have great appeal because it has a certain
"sound." Some good examples: The owner of
Carvel Ice Cream whose obviously non-
professional, deep-throated gravely voice gave the
product instant identification. And: remember the
twang of Titus Moody for Pepperidge Farm.

80. All this sounds great to me. Can I get away with just radio advertising?
A: No way. Radio is strictly complimentary to your
other advertising. It reinforces, reemphasizes,
repeats the message you tell in other media. It is the
cumulative effect of all your advertising — all
carrying the same message at the same time — that
makes your advertising work for you.

YOUR TEN POINT CHECKLIST WHEN BUYING RADIO

We asked several radio salespeople what are the
most-asked questions from advertisers when they are
thinking about buying time on radio. Here are some
of the most-asked. If your fellow business people

want to know the answers before they commit the dollars, so should you.

1. What kind of music do you play?
2. How far does your signal reach?
3. How large is your audience?
4. Where is your station located on the dial? Is it AM or FM?
5. Do I have to pay anything to have a commercial made?
6. Are you rated in your market? By whom? Can I see the ratings?
7. What does "satellite" mean?
8. What does "drive time" mean?
9. How important are the jocks (radio personalities) in their time frame and will they do my commercial for me at no cost?
10. Will radio really work for my business?

WHAT MAKES A GOOD RADIO COMMERCIAL?

One that makes the customer buy. But first they have to listen. For some reason, humor plays better in radio. Perhaps because the imagination is put to work (like the Stan Freberg commercial mentioned at the beginning of this chapter.)

Every year the Clio awards choose the best advertising commercials. We chose one winner from radio to show you how humor can and does work.

(This award winner is from the Campbell-Mithun-Esty agency in Chicago.)

53

KROGER DOUBLE PRINT RADIO COMMERCIAL

Nun: You wanted to see me, Father?

Priest: Yes, Sister, I got back the pictures from the parish picnic.

Nun: Oh, so fast!

Priest: Well, I took them to Kroger.

Nun: Ah, Kroger.

Priest: You know, Kroger gives you an extra set of prints free.

Nun: Do they, now?

Priest: And the folks at Kroger say to mail the second print to someone special.

Nun: Ohh.

Priest: So, here's a shot of Mother Superior smashing a spike at the volleyball tournament.

Nun: Ooh, the colors are so vivid!

Priest: Kroger uses Kodak paper and the Kodak Colorwatch System.

Nun: You know, we should send that extra print to the Mother's brother, Father.

Priest: Her brother, Sister?

Nun: Or her mother, Father.

Priest: Fine. Here's the Deacon sliding into Home in the softball game.

Nun: This free print should go to the Brother's mother, Father.

Priest: His mother, Sister?

Nun: Or his brother, Father.

Priest: The Brother's brother? I thought he had a sister, Sister.

Nun: No, a brother, mother, and a father, Father.

Priest: Oh, and here's the finish of the three-legged race.

Nun: Ooh, Sister Ann and Brother Andrew.

Priest: Who gets the extra free print?

Nun: Well, is a Brother's sister more special than a Sister's brother?

Priest: But what about the father of the Brother and the mother of the Sister?

Nun: Aren't you being partial to the father, Father?

Priest: Well, you're pulling for the sister, Sister!

Nun: Oh, Kroger has set a task for us, sure enough.

Priest: Aye.

Nun: Figuring out who to mail that extra free print to could try the patience of a Saint.

Priest: Shall we try again?

Nun: Aye, Father.

Priest: Fine. We send the picture of the Brother...

Both: ...to the mother of the Sister...

Voice over: Double prints...at Kroger.

4

TV Or Not TV?

There was a time, not so very long ago, that the person with a small business watched but never thought of advertising on TV. The reason was simple: it cost too much.

This was the time when your TV set broadcast only three channels - one from each of the major networks. Yes, you could buy commercials from the local network affiliate station that would broadcast only to the local audience but the cost was still prohibitive - especially if you were near big city audiences.

And then, along came cable. Now available in 60 percent of American homes.

Now, instead of choosing between one of three channels to watch, the audience can choose from literally hundreds!

Now, you can use TV to pinpoint the channel you feel most of your customers (or potential customers) will watch.

Now you can *customerize* what you have to sell to what a specific customer watching a specific channel wants to buy.

And best of all, now *you can afford it!*

Twenty years ago only 13 percent of local advertising dollars was spent on TV. Most of the rest went to newspaper. Today, that percentage is over 20 percent and could account for nearly 30 percent by the year 2000.

Today, your local TV station will come to your place of business and make you part of the commercial as well as showing what your business looks like. Most times this is included in the rates you pay — especially if you agree to run a certain number of commercials in a certain amount of time.

TV's strong advantage is reaching so many homes so quickly on a one-on-one basis. That's you — up there on the screen — in the flesh talking to people in their living rooms all over your selling area. Sometime during the day nine out of ten of your potential customers are watching something on TV. (Including the annual 30,000 plus commercials). Comparison: Fewer than eight out of ten adults read the newspaper.

In our brief forays into TV, we did our own announcing of new products, sales and special events. These appearances were invariably followed by people stopping us on the street and saying, "Saw you on TV last night."

TV connotes a glamorous image. Yes, yes, there are those Crazy Charlie auto and appliance ads with screaming salespeople or owners parading around with animals—but, generally, TV exposure creates an aura of interest from the consumer not discernible with radio, newspaper or direct mail.

TV, more than any other medium, gives you instant

identification. That's why most politicians spend most of their money on TV ads. It gives them an identity of who they are and what they say they will do far quicker than any other medium. Many politicians today use TV as their ONLY advertising medium!

TV combines sight, sound, motion and emotion for powerful selling.

TV is rated by most people as exciting, authoritative and exerting more influence on their buying decisions.

TV's viewing audience is growing every year — about 5 to 7 hours per day or more than on all other media combined!

TV, today, is more and more competitive as more and more channels open. We have compiled 20 suggestions to consider, think about and finally do when putting together your first — or next — advertisement on TV.

THE 20 RULES FOR TV ADVERTISING

81. **The picture must tell the story.** Remember Ogilvy's theory: "Can you turn off the sound and still know what's being sold?" If you can't...try again.

82. **Show the product.** Car commercials showing trees, grass and rivers don't sell cars as Infinti learned. Blue jeans commercials showing young people in amorous positions attracts attention but

does it sell jeans? They may sell an image — but is it YOUR image and, more important, your product? When a local baby furniture store wanted the community to know who they were and what they sold, the local cable station did a commercial showing different parts of their store with cribs, beds, strollers. They received almost instant identification!

83. **Demonstrate how your product or service works.** You see this on the fast-growing infomercial craze. How the cloth with the special ingredient removes scratches on your car. How throwing all your vegetables and fruit into a high geared mixer makes a delicious drink. If your chairs are made of unbreakable steel, throw them around the studio (remember the commercials of the gorilla throwing the Samsonite luggage around his cage?). Visual effects are so effective because TV is . . . visual!

84. **Don't worry about the audience "zapping" your commercial.** Much is written about the fast draw of the TV pad in switching channels when an ad appears. The Television Bureau of Advertising did an in depth research on this perception. Result: It's a minor problem. Nearly 83 percent of the audience say they NEVER switch channels during a commercial break.

85. **Use testimonials.** Yes, we've said this also works in every other media but they *really* appear real on TV. Suggestion: Do NOT write a script for customers

who agree to say nice things about you. Let them say anything they want. You can edit out the "ummms" and "ahhhs" and extraneous phrases. And if the people you choose do NOT look like models or professionals, ...terrific! That means they look more "real." Paying the extra money for a well-known personality means the viewer will remember the personality — not necessarily your product.

86. Don't mention the competition. This is a growing phenomena in many of today's TV ads. "Our product is better than (name of competitive product)." The problem is that many of the viewers only remember your competitor's name!

87. Tight close-ups of the face are dramatic. No extraneous arms, legs, props to get in the way of your face (or the announcer you choose) talking directly to the consumer. Very effective. Just like selling face-to-face.

88. Mention the name of your company or product up front. Then repeat it again and again and again and most especially at the end.

89. TV is the most emotional of all media. I watch the Hallmark Hall of Fame productions mainly for the commercials. Each is a 30 or 60 second piece of art. The morning after the show it often seems that as many people talk about the commercials as the show.

90. Be wary of TV salespeople who try to sell you on "recall." Many will show you statistics saying how many people remembered a specific TV commercial. Your follow-up question: "I don't care how many *remembered* the commercial. I care how many *bought from* the commercial."

91. Grab the viewer's attention quickly. No different from the headline on the print ad. The same four or five seconds is all the time the viewer will give you before they decide whether to watch the rest of the commercial (read the rest of the copy).

92. Have a beginning, middle and end. Think of each commercial as a mini story. The viewer should be able to follow along and see the problem you present and how you solve it. They must not only see the offer you make but also the benefit they receive.

93. Avoid expensive props and settings. Watch commercials on your TV on national networks and you will see very effective copy only commercials. Aetna insurance ads used only words on a screen and voices in the background. Very effective.

94. Use clever film techniques sparingly. Otherwise you call attention to the editing and not the product.

95. Certain products sell very well on TV. That's

why you see a lot of soap, beer and car commercials. A study by Bruskin Associates Market Research asked TV viewers questions about buying their next car. The overwhelming majority knew the car they wanted but six out of ten did NOT know where they would go to buy. Nearly 80 percent said TV is the medium that tells them about automobiles. So if you're selling cars. . . .

96. Be careful what you say. Somebody's listening. Every word counts. Your audience is often listening when they're not watching. Your viewer may leave the room during the commercial but can still hear the words.

97. Don't plan on revisions. They take time. And money. Your salesperson will review what you want to say ahead of time. Most will give you "storyboards" to look at which show you a sketch of the picture and the words to be spoken. Look at everything very carefully. Ask yourself if your story is being told in a persuasive manner with lots of benefits to the reader. When you see the finished commercial and ask to do certain parts over you are asking to spend much more money and much more time than changing words on a radio spot or copy in a newspaper ad. It's expensive.

98. Schedule your ads any season other than summer. Here's why: TV viewing decreases about 17 percent in summer but you pay the same for your ad! The exceptions of course are if you are

advertising summer-only products: patio furniture,
bathing suits, suntan lotion. But if your product is
year–round, place most of your ad dollars when
most people are watching.

99. Be wary of humor. Yes, they make people laugh
but the big question is "Do they make people buy?"
People buy for dozens of reasons that include but
are not limited to saving time, saving money,
making money, to protect their family, for comfort,
health and praise. But people don't buy because
you made them laugh. It was Claude Hopkins, the
father of modern advertising who proclaimed,
"People don't buy from clowns." Yes, humor
attracts attention, make people feel good (which
is just a half step from buying that which-makes-
them-feel-good) but you have to be very, very
careful since what makes one person laugh makes
another person feel uncomfortable, uneasy and
unhappy with what you're trying to sell.

100. Make it newsworthy. A tactic we emphasize in
every form of advertising because it works in every
form of advertising. Is there a way you can tie your
product/business into a local event? Special
Olympics? Scholastic Athletics? Community fund
drives? That association gives your business an
added lustre and creates a positive image.

5

Dollar for Dollar, Nothing Returns as Much to Your Business as Direct Mail

The year was 1964. We had a little children's clothing business in Atlantic City, New Jersey. Our annual volume was so small we could not afford conventional advertising. However, we did have names and addresses of a few hundred customers. We decided to send them a mimeographed letter once a month on merchandise on sale just for them.

For a very small cost, we doubled our business.

I wrote a story about what we were doing and sent it to *Direct Marketing* magazine. The editor called and said he would buy the story and "since we believe retail direct mail is the coming revolution, would you like to write a monthly column on retail direct mail?"

"I certainly would, " I replied, hung up and turned to my wife and asked, "What's retail direct mail?"

The "coming revolution" of retail direct mail predicted 30 years ago turned out to be scattered shots by untrained marksmen using ancient weapons. Only within the past few years has there been an attempt to encourage, educate and embolden the small businessperson to use direct mail in their business.

"Retail direct mail" remains, for the most part, an orphan. Known about, sometimes mentioned, but rarely invited to the party. Look through the program of any marketing convention held in the U.S. (or anywhere in the world). Trying to find anyone speaking on retail direct mail is searching for the proverbial needle in a haystack. This, despite the fact that more money is spent on direct mail than is spent on magazines, radio, billboards and advertising T-shirts —all put together!

So who's spending all the money on direct mail? The large catalogue companies. The big department stores. Look through your morning mail and see the advertisements from the office supply folks, computer companies, book publishers. But not much from the local small businessperson. Doesn't make sense.

Today small businesspeople still spend only about 2¢ out of their advertising dollars on direct mail. Only about five percent of U.S. retailers are using any kind of retail direct mail.

Some revolution. . .

The small businessman or woman contributes up to 80 percent of the employment and a major share of any country's gross national revenue. Who's teaching them, showing them, encouraging them to do retail direct mail — their most valuable weapon to survive and succeed in an increasingly competitive economy?

Now, we cannot, in this one brief chapter tell you all about direct mail and how it works. That would be like the woman who called me one morning and said, "I just opened a dress shop and I want to use direct mail, can you tell me how it works in the next few minutes?"

Well, uh . . . no.

What I CAN tell you is that, **dollar for dollar, nothing returns as much to your business as direct mail.**

We DID write a basic book on what-it-is and how-it-works with our good friend and award winning direct mail talent Ken Erdman called "The Do It Yourself Direct Mail Handbook."

The reason for that book was because somewhere, sometime, somehow there was a small business person that said, "I'd like to do direct mail. . . but I just don't know how."

That's true. The salespeople from the newspaper, radio, TV, magazines all come in to see you with layouts, designs, copy, jingles. All you have to do is sign the bottom line and they take care of the rest.

But not direct mail. That's you.

Can you start without a 12 week college course?

Can you be effective without reading a dozen books on how-to-do-it?

Is there a simple, easy, uncomplicated method that will work?

The answer to those questions is yes, yes and yes.

The answer is Direct Mail. Which is the **most** effective use of *Customerization*.

Through the years we've received phone calls and letters asking about what works and what doesn't. What's important and what's not. We have narrowed those queries down to the 20 Most-Asked-Questions-About-Direct-Mail (...*and the answers*).

You can start off by simply building a list of your present customers names and addresses. When you have a few hundred, write them a letter telling them what's new in your business, what's different, exciting and unusual that just arrived and, oh yes, you've included some special offers just for them. NOT advertised anyplace else.

Here are the 20 Most-Asked-Questions-About-Direct-Mail (. . .*and the answers.*)

101. What are the advantages of direct mail over any other advertising?

A: Two big advantages:

1. *Selectivity.* You can mail to whom you want to mail. You can't tell the local radio or TV station, "Next time you run my commercial, only run it in this part of town 'cause that's where my customers live. Don't run it anywhere else." Can't do it. Some newspapers do offer some selective zip code mailings for special prices but you're still surrounded by all those other ads.

2. *Measurability.* Ed Mayer, one of the early gurus of direct marketing said it well, "Direct Marketing is a 'what' medium not a 'why' medium. If I send out 1,000 mailers and 100 people show up, I know 'what' happened — I had a 10 percent return on mailing list. But I don't necessarily know 'why'."

102. What's a direct mail piece made up of?

A: Three parts: The list, the offer and the creative. Of these three, the list is the most important. A "rough" gauge of the importance of each might look like this:

List	50%
Offer	35%
Creative	15%

This breakdown makes the creative people like me very unhappy. But I know it's true. If you have the best offer in the world, but you send it to the wrong list, you will have terrible results.

If you have the best list but you send them a bad offer, you will have terrible results.

And if your creative is designed by an award-winning artist on the most expensive paper and sealed with hot red wax and is mailed to the wrong list with the wrong offer you will have disastrous guaranteed money-losing results. So, if the most important part of your mailer is the list then where do you find this "list"?

It begins with the customers you have. Every time anyone spends any money with you, write down his or her name and address and telephone number. If possible, see if you can find out even more information:

- Birthday (month and day only. People don't want you to know their age);
- Clothing size (if you're a clothing store);
- Favorite artist (if you sell prints);
- Favorite foods (if you're a food store)

Well, you get the idea. The more information, the

better your results. Knowing something about your customer is as important as knowing everything about your product.

103. How do I know the people still live where I'm sending the mail?

A: Good question. Especially since one out of five people move every year. If you send something first class mail, the post office will return your letter with the corrected address at no charge. If you send something out third class mail, the postage is cheaper but you pay for each corrected address.

104. Will I receive better results if I personalize my mailings?

A: Not always. Here's why: if your computer prints the customer's name several times on one page, most people will know it's a computer letter. It's far, far more important to have a *personal* letter than a *personalized* letter. What's that mean? This: your letter should be friendly comfortable, one-on-one as if they were in the room and the two of you were having a conversation. That's much, much more believable than printing the name several times in the letter which can be not only intimidating but feel like an invasion of privacy.

105. What's the difference between first class and third class mail?

A: In a word: money. Third class is cheaper. BUT. . . third class arrives much later. You have to figure about 10 days. Often more. If you are working on a

tight deadline mail first class. Especially if you have
a small list. The difference in postage for 1,000
mailing pieces is only about $100. Not worth the
savings.

106. People receive lots of mail. How can I make sure they see and read mine?

A: Your customers will open your mailer. If they are
not customers of yours, try something different:
Mail in a box, a tube, an oversized or colorful
envelope. In the first few seconds your customers
handle a mailer, they make the decision whether
they will open it. Hand write the address. Use the
BACK of the envelope for one-more-reason to read
what you sent.

What they'll always read: A letter addressed to
them personally. Especially handwritten. Great
example: A "thank you" after they have bought
something from your business will be remembered.

107. How fast will I know if my mailer worked or not?

A: Within two weeks after your customers receive
the mailer.

108. How often should I mail to my customers?

A: At least four times a year. We discovered sending
mailings to our top 500 customers once a month
was not too much. We discovered sending mailings
to our top 500 customers *twice* a month was not too
much. Great list. As long as we made it a great offer
we would average a 20 percent response!

109. What's the most important word to use in my headline?
A: If I had to pick one, it would be "free." Use it. Often. Say "free." Then say "complimentary." Then say "no charge."

110. Shall I accept only a check with the order?
A: No. The more ways you give the customer to pay, the higher the response. That means check or credit cards or C.O.D or so much down and so much a month.

111. Are there certain words that make the reader want to keep on reading?
A: Sure. Here are a few: *new, save, guarantee, hurry, wanted, announcing, easy, offer expires* (date), *limited offer, discover* and *you*. John Caples, direct marketing guru, once examined the most successful ads ever written. He found the word "you" appeared in nearly half the winning ads. How about "Free for you." That's good . . .

112. I read somewhere that a real stamp pulls better than printed stamps, that a smaller envelope is better than a bigger envelope, that long copy out pulls short copy (or was it short copy outpulls long copy?) that...
A: Stop. None of that matters very much. Go back to step #1: The list, the offer, the creative.

113. What percentage of returns should you receive from your direct mail?

A: It depends.

It depends on how much you are spending and how much you are receiving back. If you want to sell a Rolls Royce and you receive only a 1% return on your mailings it is more than enough to pay for the mailing and make a nice profit because the cost of the item is so high. Lower priced items need higher percentage of response.

A rule of thumb is that your business can usually expect a return of around 10 percent if your mailer is going to your regular customers who expect to receive direct mail from you on a regular basis.

No other advertising medium gives you an exact measurement. But when you send out a direct mail piece, you'll know in a few days whether or not your mailer worked. That's why people "test" their mailings.

We once did a sale and mailed out gift certificates. The customers had to fill out their name and address on the gift certificate when they came to the store. We received 15% of the certificates back. Next time, we pre-printed the names on the gift certificates and the response rate jumped to 25%!

I love David Ogilvy's story of the time his brother Francis wrote a letter in Greek to the headmasters of private schools selling cooking stoves. When some wrote back they could not read Greek, he sent them another letter – in Latin!

114. Is there a trick I can use to increase response?
A: Here's one that works: Involvement. Have your customers fill in something, tear open something,

use a "yes" or "no" label. Something!

115. Will premiums bring in more business?

A: Yes! Examples are all around you: Look at the cereal boxes and the special "premiums" you can have if you send in box tops. (Anyone want a slightly used Buck Rogers decoder ring? Or am I giving away my age?)

We used to go to Helsinki, Finland every January for "Vateva" — their annual fall and winter "fashion show." The four of us would usually travel SAS Airlines. One day I saw a full page ad in a travel magazine saying if I took Finnair to Finland, they would give me a notebook computer that would list telephone numbers and addresses and other information...free.

We canceled our tickets on SAS and bought tickets on Finnair.

Why: Because of the premium.

Consider offering a premium on your next mailing piece. We were able to increase the return 5 percent on our mailing piece for New Year's Day — our biggest sale day of the year — when we offered a Free Trip For Two . . . to somewhere people wanted to go: New Orleans, Disney World. We made a barter deal with our travel agent ("we advertise your agency in our mailer, you give us a terrific price on the trip") and our cost was only about $100. But what a dramatic difference in response to our mailer! By simply adding another "premium."

116. What's the first thing people read in a letter?

A: Whatever you put on the upper right hand part of your letter. That's where your customer's eye goes first. Siegfried Vogele, one of the world's experts in direct marketing methods is professor of Direct Marketing in Munich, Germany. He has done extensive "eye" tests on what people look at first, second and so on when they receive your mailing piece. First they want to know who is writing to them. Then they look at how the letter is addressed. And then their eye jumps to who signed the letter and the next thing they read is...the P.S. (surprise, surprise). They do not go back to the beginning of the letter until they read the P.S. ("Hmmmmmm, I wonder what they forgot to put in the letter that they had to add at the end?") So make sure the P.S. repeats the big benefit you put up front which they won't get around to reading until they've read the P.S.

117. When's the best time to mail?
A: January. That's why you receive all those big packages from publishing houses telling you how many millions of dollars you have won. THEY know January is the best month for results. And to answer your next question, the worst month to mail is usually June. Because vacations start or weddings happen or school closes or . . . Another bad time is December unless your mailer has to do with gift-giving. Christmas gift giving takes precedence over everything else. Just remember you're fighting the mailbox glut of thousands of other marketers who are also selling gift ideas.

75

118. Do testimonials work?

A: Yes. If they relate specifically to the product. The BEST testimonials are from people who have used your product. Give their names and their cities to show they are real people.

119. What if I get back a terrific response to my mailer? Can I make the exact same offer to the exact same list a few weeks later?

A: Sure. Here's why: On the average, sending the same offer to the same list (to those who did NOT buy the first time around) will return half of your first time response. So, add up your costs and your sales. If one-half the response still gives you a profit. . . go for it!

120. How can I start?

A: Two ways: 1. Save the direct mail pieces you receive that captured your attention and copy the best ideas. 2. Call your postmaster. Set up a meeting with him or her. Start off by stating, "I want to do direct mail for my business. Can you help me?"

6

TELEPHONE MARKETING: REACH OUT & SELL SOMETHING

Question: Where are most advertising dollars spent?

( ) Newspaper
( ) Television
( ) Radio
( ) Direct Mail
( ) Telephone
( ) Magazines
( ) Yellow Pages
( ) Billboards

If you answered anything else besides "telephone"....you're wrong.

More than 70 billion dollars was spent annually on telemarketing in the early 1990s. This is a form of advertising you should at least think about using.

In this chapter we are talking about using the telephone as a marketing tool working with your present customers: when they call you or you call them.

Consider this fact: it costs *at least* five times more to get a new customer than to keep a current one. And one way to keep your present customers is to call them.

When you call your present customer, you are talking to a specific target: someone who knows you and has spent money with you and will appreciate your call because you are bringing them information. Your phone call is to someone rather than to anyone.

Why is so much money spent on telephone marketing?

1. It is interactive. (You and the customer talk to one another)
2. It is responsible. (The customer finds out up front, at once if you can fulfill their needs and wants.)
3. It is synergistic. (You can "open the door" for sending a catalogue, merchandise or having a salesperson call.)
4. Almost everyone has a phone. Everyone does NOT subscribe to the paper or listen to the TV and radio at the time you want them to listen.
5. If you call someone after you have mailed them something, you can increase the results from your mailer five to ten times!

Telemarketing has not grown because it is cheap. It isn't. An overwhelming majority of the phone calls you place (outbound) don't reach the customer the first time around. Telemarketing has grown so quickly because the customer wants fast, convenient and economical ways to buy what you have to sell.

Limit your calls to people who are current customers. It's less expensive than cold calling and will result in more sales. And your customers won't complain about intrusive and annoying phone calls from strangers.

Selling by telephone works two ways: Inbound and Outbound.

Inbound means someone calls you.

Outbound means you call someone.

Here's some information on how each works followed by a list of 20 rules for telephone marketing. Let's start with Inbound. That's when you hear the phone ring.

INBOUND

• **When you pick up the phone, you start selling.**
The Rule of First Impressions begins when someone answers your phone. What do they "sound" like? What's the person on the other end want to hear? This: That they reached the right place. And the name of the person they are talking to.

• **Nothing is a problem.**
Many times customers will call with a problem they have with one of your products. Not delivered. Not performing. Not what was ordered. Most people are uncomfortable calling to complain. They're preconditioned from a previous experience or the horror stories they read or heard and are convinced you will give them a difficult time. What a shock (and surprise) to have you say, "We'll take care of that for you. What would you like?"

Think about it. What real difference does it make to

you anyway? A refund, a replacement, even a lost of money? What you have to think about is the "lifetime value of the customer." Is this telephone marketing? You bet it is!

George Walther, in his excellent book, *Phone Power*, suggests you eliminate certain negative phrases when you're talking to a customer and substitute positive phrases.

Do NOT say, "I can't." Say *when* you **can.**

Do NOT say, "I'll try." That means you may or may not.

Do NOT say, "I'm not sure." DO say "I'll get back to you with an answer." And then, "If I call you within an hour, is that OK?"

Many calls are made to ask if you have a special item, if you can deliver or mail a product (yes, yes, of course you can. *"Tell us what you want and the answer is yes."*).

After taking the order, suggest something else. But make that something "special."

We once helped create a food catalogue for a retailer. When we received the catalogue, we called for an order. They were polite, accurate and thanked us. We then called the owner and said, "Every time someone takes an order suggest something ELSE for them to buy. Something NOT in the catalogue and is a special price for this week only. You will sell that extra item to one out of ten who call."

He called us back a few weeks later and told us we were wrong. One out of five bought.

OUTBOUND

• **Make four phone calls a day.**
Each of your salespeople have a list of their favorite customers. (And if they don't have, start that today!). This little black book has the customer's name, address, telephone number and the kind of merchandise they like.

Simply calling them up and letting them know **what-they-like just arrived**, will be flattering and will automatically produce sales.

Simply calling them up and letting them know about **a sale ahead of time** will be flattering and automatically produce sales.

Simply calling them up and **reminding them about a birthday or holiday** will be flattering and automatically produce sales.

The big advantage for your business is that all these calls are made by people presently on your payroll. They make these calls during "down" time, when they are not taking care of customers in your business.

The bigger advantage: Telemarketing is the most direct form of *Customerization*. You are giving a specific message to a specific customer for a specific item you know they want. You can't get more customized than that!

20 RULES FOR TELEMARKETING

121. Answer the phone quickly!

81

If you let it ring more than 3 times, the person calling is annoyed.

122. Say who-you-are. Speak clearly. Say your name easily. Most people talk too fast and the listener, hearing a non-familiar name, doesn't quickly associate who-you-are.

123. Say who you're with. Like this: "Good morning. This is Tom Jenkins from the Gordon's shops."

124. Don't keep me on hold too long. Most people are annoyed to be put "on hold." More people are further annoyed by listening to canned music. Try to answer the person's question immediately or offer to call them back with an answer. They'll appreciate the fact that you honor their time. How long is too long? Longer than a minute is too long. Holding onto a phone for a minute equates into five minutes in the customer's mind.

125. If a customer is complaining, don't interrupt. Let customers finish what they want to say before you offer a solution. You should, however, let them know you're still there with little phrases like, "I see" or "I understand" or a simple "uh huh" . That way the customer will feel you're concerned. After you hang up, drop them a note to confirm what you promised. Boy, will they be impressed.
126. Use the customer's name. A quick and easy way to build a comfortable relationship is to mention the customer's name while talking to him or her. This

personalization will diffuse anger.

Now, if you want to sell something to your customer . . .

127. Give your staff an outline. The 1-2-3 key points they should use when talking to customers. Here's why: You are condensing a selling story into the least possible words with the most possible benefits. Doing this "off the cuff" will not work. You must prepared ahead of time. Bob Hope once said, "The best ad-lib is the rehearsed ad lib."

Some of your salespeople may say they "are not actors." Remind them they use certain phrases all the time in their every day face-to-face selling.

Don't use a written script salespeople have to memorize because it will sound like a written script they have memorized. Just give them the key points and let them take it from there. They must have the option of changing words or phrases that "sound more like me." The important goal is to make it sound "natural."

128. Tell. Don't sell. When you sell, the person on the other end of the lines hears the "sound of selling" in your voice. When you sound friendly on the phone, the person listening to you is more receptive to what you have to say. Relax. Remember: Everyone likes to buy. But no one wants to be sold.

129. Use the four C's. Be Clear, Concise, Conversational and Convincing.

O.K, the phone is ringing and your potential buyer picks up the phone ...

130. Say who you are and what you want up front.
When you call a customer do NOT say you are a salesperson for your company.

Instead say, "Hi. This is Murray. Is Mrs. Walsh there?" Most of the time you'll get Mrs. Walsh. If the person asks, "Who's calling?" THEN say who you are where you're from and why you're calling.

131. QUICK! Give a benefit! "I'm calling to tell you about the winter sale we're having at Gordon's and, since you're a good customer, I wanted you to know about it before it's advertised." Yes, yes, of course, your telephone call IS an advertisement. But not in the "accepted" newspaper/radio/TV tradition of advertising.

Now you've told them you're from a store they know. Where they shop.

Now you've told them a special reason they should keep on listening

132. Explain the benefit and give a cut-off date.
That creates desire and immediacy. "We're offering 20 percent off everything in the store during this sale. The sale starts on Monday and will last only one week. That's why we wanted you to have this advance notice."

133. Deliver the entire message quickly.
Don't waste your customer's time. Come to the

main selling feature right away.

134. Ask Questions. Don't just keep on talking. The magic word is "involvement." Can't do that unless you ask a question: "I know you like Calvin Klein clothing. Would you like to know what's on sale in your size?" Rare is the person who will turn down THAT offer. And then....LISTEN! Many salespeople feel they have to keep on talking, like background music in a movie. But with silence comes orders.

135. Ask for the order. "Would you like me to put one aside for you today? Oh yes, they also make a marvelous gift."

136. Offer add-ons "In addition to the 20 percent off sale, we're having a half price sale on six foot wool scarves. They normally sell for $20 but you can have them on sale for half price. Only $10. They come in five colors." They will immediately tell you if they want the scarf and will ask you the colors. Great. You've established a dialogue.

"The colors are navy, white, brown, camel, and black. Which color do you prefer? " This is the "Not if, but which" technique. Give the customer a choice between something and something. Not something and nothing.

137. Handling objections. If the customer isn't interested in the half price scarf (or other great buy you offer) accept the turn-down gracefully and ask, "Is there anything else you would like me to put

85

aside for you to look at when you come to the store? There's no obligation to buy. We just want to make sure our best customers have best choices."

138. Read back what they ordered. The customer will appreciate you are confirming what they said to you especially since they can't see and sign the sales receipt.

139. Guarantee. Tell them they must be satisfied or you will take the merchandise back. This makes the customer feel more comfortable when buying.

140. The close. Sign off with a pleasant goodbye and a "thank you" whether or not the customer bought anything. Last impressions count almost as much as first impressions.

7

SPEAK UP!
(OR: FIND OUT WHAT THE CUSTOMER WANTS TO LISTEN TO AND GIVE IT TO THEM.)

A recent survey asked the question: "What do you fear most?" The top two answers were death and public speaking.

And public speaking came in first!

Somewhere, somehow, sometime, you will be asked to give a talk. It may be a simple introduction to a friend receiving an honor. Or a 20 minute talk to the local service club. Or addressing a convention of your colleagues on the techniques that contributed to your success.

If you are like most people, this will make you very nervous and reluctant and fearful.

It is a fear you should overcome because speaking gives you the opportunity at little or no cost to be the best public relations person your business can possibly have: you.

That's how it began for me.

Through the years I have given thousands of speeches. I travel more than 200,000 miles a year around the world talking on marketing, advertising and promotion.

And so, I set aside this chapter to give you 20 ideas to make your next speech, or your first speech, successful. Although most or all of these ideas are known and practiced by professional speakers they are also important for the speaker just-starting-out.

Now you might say, "Gee, I don't want to be a speaker." But a speech can be great advertising for little or no cost. A short 20 minute luncheon talk to the Rotary, Lions, name-your-local-club will do that for you. They are ALWAYS interested in FREE speakers. Your speech can tell who you are, how you got started and what your business does. Then, you can leave some handouts with gift certificates they can redeem within the next week or two.

This can be an excellent public relations tool to bring unpaid advertising and attention to your business.

You have to always be selling your business. Think of speaking as just another advertising tool.

Like most things you try for the first time, the first time is the most difficult. You will be frustrated, feel inadequate, think you are making a fool of yourself. These are natural fears. But how about the first time you bought merchandise for your business? The first time you hired someone. The first time you did....anything?

You learn by doing. And the fifth or sixth time you give the same talk, it will be as natural as telling me about what-you-do when you invite me over for coffee at your home.

How do you give a speech? It begins with preparation.

THE 20 RULES FOR GIVING A SPEECH

141. Prepare.

The secret to success in speaking is preparation, preparation, and more preparation. The more you know about your audience, the more successful your presentation.

When writing or giving a speech, follow this simple three step rule:

1. Say what you are going to say.
2. Say it.
3. Say what you said.

When you make an important point, repeat that sentence. The audience will then know that it is important and remember.

Even when speaking to local organizations, ask ahead of time for their handbook. Find out their goals, the names of their officers. Relate your talk - especially in the beginning - to who they are and what they do. If you begin by speaking about their organization and what they do, you strike a responsive chord right up front.

I once met a speaker who was amazed by the amount of research I demanded for each show. He said, "The trouble with you is you overprepare."

I thought about that later and realized the alternative was to *under*prepare. Most of the time the audience will never know you don't know anything about them. But if you don't prepare, your audience will think, "What the heck does this have to do with MY business?"

The successful speech means you *Customerize* your message for your audience.

As a first time speaker you must find a way to relate what you're talking about to your audience. Otherwise they will not be interested. Would you?

142. The introduction.

Write it out yourself. In capital letters and double spaced so it's easy to read. It should be, AT MOST, one page long. Half a page is better. If you don't write out an introduction, you never know what will happen.

One time I was working with Ray Considine, a professional motivational speaker. The setting was a retail food convention in New Mexico. The person who introduced us walked to the microphone and said: "Our next speakers really need no introduction so I won't give them one. Here they are!"

And he walked off the stage without even saying our names.

Ray and I dashed to the front, grabbed the two microphones and introduced one another....

I was tempted to use an old speaker's joke when that kind of terrible introduction happens. It goes like this:

"I want to thank (NAME) for that introduction. We've known one another for -what is it - must be ten years. In all that time there isn't anything I

wouldn't do for him. And there isn't anything he
wouldn't do for me. And so we've gone through life
doing nothing for one another."

I could have used it but I didn't. Because the
audience would have disliked me more than the
introducer.

143. Have a great beginning and a great ending.

Do that and you are almost guaranteed a successful
talk.

Remember the old story: you never have a second
chance to make a first impression? It's true. I work
very hard on my show openings and closings.

Many speakers open with a joke. O.K. if you're a
joke teller. But that requires timing and the ability to
deliver a joke. I personally like to tell stories rather
than jokes.

You need something easy, comfortable up front to
put your audience at ease. If you're comfortable,
they're comfortable. If you're ill at ease, they're ill at
ease.

A good way to start: poke fun at yourself.
Audiences don't like pompous people impressed
with themselves. If you make fun of yourself in the
beginning of your talk, the audience will
subconsciously say, "Hey, this guy's all right."

I often begin following my introduction which has
a lot of my accomplishments through the years with
this story:

"I hope you are all impressed with that marvelous
introduction. It's all true. I am brilliant, talented,
creative. And I would like to prove that to you.

91

I joined my brother-in-law and sister-in-law in their business 35 years ago. They were doing $15,000 a YEAR in business. Absolutely true.

In just one year — because I was there putting together all the creative, imaginative, talented ideas I am capable of — in twelve months — I was able to increase that business from $15,000 a year to (pause) $16,000 a year... So I hope you're all impressed with the talent you see in front of you today."

144. Be enthusiastic.

An audience will enjoy almost anything you say as long as they see you are having a good time saying it. One of the best speakers we know, Bill Gove, says, "The messenger is more important than the message."

Does that surprise you? It shouldn't. Think of the times you have gone to meetings and heard someone drone on in a monotone about some subject. Your mind wanders, you find yourself getting sleepy. You just don't care. But have the speaker be enthusiastic and excited about his subject and you find yourself becoming enthusiastic as well.

Speaker Ty Boyd says, "You must have energy, fire in your belly, enthusiasm. Not necessarily jumping up and down telling funny stories energy but REAL energy. You can see it the speakers' eyes, feel it in their words, sense it in their presence. Even when they whisper."

145. Check equipment ahead of time.

If you find yourself speaking more than

occasionally, you are doing enough speaking to prepare a list of equipment you need to send to the program coordinator. You constantly have to check ahead of time to make sure what-you-asked-for-is-what-you-get.

Using visuals WILL make your speech more effective. Your points also last longer. Here's why: we learn about 10% by hearing and about 75% by seeing (the rest by tasting, touching and smelling).

People generally remember about one-fifth of what they hear, about one third of what they see. But if they both hear **and** see something - they'll remember about half of the presentation.

You can use a blackboard (for a small audience), a flip chart (for a slightly bigger audience), overhead projectors, (for up to 150 people in the room), slides (for almost any size audience) and videotapes. The first few are inexpensive. The last two are more expensive. And be careful of OVERvisualizing your presentation. It's similar to reading your speech. If you have to read it, why not simply hand out printed copies for everyone to take home? If every sentence becomes something you have to draw, sketch, show on a screen, you can videotape the show and not appear in person.

Visual aids are what they say they are; an "aid" to your talk. They complement, supplement but do not replace what you have to say.

But even if you put together a list of needed equipment, you can't list . . . everything!

I once worked in Auckland, New Zealand for a group of retailers. I sent detailed instructions on how we wanted the room set up, the audio-visual requirements, the size of the screen, the equipment needed.

The organizer for the event showed me around the room an hour before the program began, beaming with pride as he checked off every item on my list.

We looked around and asked, 'How many people do you expect?":

"About 250," he said.

"Well, everything I asked you for on the list is here," I said, " but there's just one thing...where are the chairs?"

"CHAIRS?" he said, "CHAIRS? There was nothing in your list about having chairs!"

He quickly contacted a local undertaker who came through with chairs.

Hey, you can't remember *everything!*

Speaking of chairs . . . check with the program chairman to see how many people they expect. If they say 200, count the chairs assembled. (There will probably be 500.) Persuade him to have staff take down at least 200 chairs and put them in the back of the room. Speaking to an audience scattered around a room full of empty seats means your talk will never receive a rating from the audience of more than one on a scale of one to five. Here's why: When the audience is packed together they function as a unit. When they're scattered around, they function as individuals. They don't laugh or applaud as easily.

I've always believed the greatest audience to speak to is in a room with 200 chairs and 300 people.

One time I went to see a famous financial speaker work in my home town, Atlantic City. He was speaking to the New Jersey Insurance Agents Association. I went into the room and saw there were more than 500 seats. I checked with the registration desk, asked how many people were signed in and they said "150.'"

I ran into the room, contacted the speaker and said, "Do you know there are only 150 people registered for this whole convention! That means you'll have less than 100 here. And there are 500 chairs. Quick! Let's take them down and put them in the back of the room."

He patted me on the shoulder condescendingly and said, "Don't worry, Murray, I like to work the room."

"Work the room?" What did THAT mean?

He began his program and I counted the audience: 23 people. They were seated all over that room among the 500 chairs.

Nothing daunted, our brave speaker, ran up and down the aisles for the whole 60 minute talk, addressing empty chairs as though they were full.

He saw, in HIS mind's eye — a full auditorium. The audience stared at him, hypnotized, wondering what he was doing.

I knew what he was doing. He was "working the room." I left before he finished. I'm the kind of guy that turns off the TV set when they show earthquakes, typhoons or people starving in a foreign land. This was another disaster I didn't want to see . . .

95

Don't forget basics: Is there water near the podium in case your throat gets dry halfway through your talk? Try the microphone. See the lighting. If the house lights are programmed to be off when you're speaking, and your only light is from a small podium lamp, your audience will not see you (and not listen). If you use slides, go through them all ahead of time to make sure they are right side up and visible! (Note: If you use slides, make them all horizontal. Fits the screen better.)

If you are using a remote clicker to move your slides, have a back up "hard wire" clicker. Here's why:

I was doing a show for Piggly Wiggly supermarkets in a hotel in Charlotte, North Carolina. I was halfway through the show when my slides began to move and I had not touched the wireless clicker! This continued until I stopped the show and had a new clicker installed, wired directly to the projector. It wasn't until my program was over that I discovered there was another program being given in the next door auditorium. They were also using a remote control. The problem: both remotes were hooked to the same radio frequency. Whenever the next door speaker clicked his remote control, *my tray moved!*

Have someone else use the microphone and listen to him from different parts of the room. What sounds good to you on stage has a completely different tone in the audience. Get out there and . . . listen.

146. Speak for the appointed time. Only.

If you are told you will speak for 30 minutes, speak for 30 minutes. Take your watch off, put it on the podium as your guide. The audience can't see it there. If you leave it on your wrist, you'll have to look at it. And the audience wonders if you (1) are bored with them or (2) have a plane to catch. In President Bush's last debate with then-Governor Clinton he looked at his watch twice. The next day's newspaper and TV stories spent more time commenting about that fact than the substance of the debates.

147. Use anecdotes.

I once asked famous speaker Bill Gove for advice on giving a "great 30 minute speech." "Easiest question I've ever been asked," said Gove. "To give a great 30 minute speech, simply tell 30 great one minute stories."

148. Don't read your speech.

Best technique is to have it memorized. Failing that, use 3 x 5 cards with large printed key points.

149. Speaking and writing are not the same.

How you talk is **not** how you write. Writing is more formal. I have transcribed my talks from cassettes recorded live. I have to edit them greatly when used for books or articles to eliminate the rambling prose that sounds natural when you talk but amateurish when written.

Speaking should be natural — like talking to a

friend. How do you do this? Rehearse! One great speaker said he always gave his speech four times: Once when he wrote it. Next when he practiced it. The third time when he actually spoke. And then fourth time when it was over and he thought of all the things he wished he'd said but didn't.

150. Look at the audience.
Make eye contact with several people while talking. Do not linger on one person (he or she will be uncomfortable). By looking at several people you achieve an intimacy that makes you more believable.

151. Listen to other speakers.
One of the ways painters learn to paint and actors learn to act and tennis players learn to play tennis is they watch the professionals. Even as a part-time speaker you can learn small techniques and ideas from watching the professionals. Not that you want to be a full-time speaker, but because you want to do the best you can possibly do.

There's another reason: the part-time speaker tends to take stories or jokes that work for professionals and use them in their presentations. If several speakers are speaking on the same program, make it a point to listen to them. One reason: you can include some points of what-they-said in YOUR talk. ("Remember earlier how Tom mentioned the importance of having a pleasant working environment. I thought about that when I decided to talk to you about...")

One better reason: you won't repeat any of the stories or jokes.

We were working at the International Marketing Symposium in Montreux, Switzerland one year and the first speaker on opening day started with this story:

"I'm glad to see a good crowd today. I was afraid when my name was on the program not many people would show up (remember: poking fun at himself). And then I remembered the story about the speaker that came out to deliver his talk and there was only one person in the audience.

Well, he figured he was there and he should do his best. He gave the entire one hour speech. When he finished the man in the audience applauded generously and the speaker said, "Thank you. And now I have to leave..."

At that point, the man in the audience jumped up and said, "Wait a minute! I'm the OTHER speaker"

It got a good laugh.

BUT: the first speaker on the next day's program with the same audience started his talk off **with the exact same joke.**

Moaning sounds in the audience...

Fortunately I heard both speakers. I started the third day's activities like this:

"I always like to tell new and original stories when I come to this convention. Now here's one you've never heard before. It seems this man came to give a speech and there was only one person in the audience..." I stopped and the laughter was twice as great as when the story was told the first time.

Imagine what would have happened if I had NOT listened to the other speakers and struggled through the SAME story. . .

152. Mingle and Learn. It's possible .

Talk to people in the audience before the show begins. Simply sit down and ask about their business, their problems. You'll be surprised how many times you can work this into your presentation. When you mention someone's name and business, the audience is very impressed. ("I was talking to Phil Stevens at lunch today. You know Phil, he has the widget factory in Franklintown. He told me how difficult it is to find trained help and the solution he came up with. He visited the local vocational school and...")

153. Vary your voice.

When you practice your speech don't become Johnny One-Note. Vary the speed of your words. And how loud you talk.

Sound is a key element in your presentation. If you are introduced and open a script, read from it in a monotonous voice, no one will listen or care and many will fall asleep...NO MATTER HOW EXCELLENT THE MESSAGE. Earl Nightingale said it well: "There are no boring subjects to talk about. Only boring speakers."

154. No off-color material. No four letter words.

Sounds like a simple admonition but I am always amazed how many speakers ignore this rule and automatically lose a percentage of their audience. You will offend someone in your audience with four letter words.

155. Use "you" as often as possible.

This rule works as well in writing to your audience as speaking to your audience. The more often you say "you" in your presentation, the more the audience feels you are talking directly to them. And the more you can eliminate the words *"I," "me"* or *"us"* and turn the sentences around so the key word is *"you"* - the more interested your audience will be in what you have to say.

156. Listen to yourself.

Tape record your talk. Then listen to it. You will cringe the first time — but mark down all the things you don't like. You'll hear all those unnecessary "Uhs . . ." and "Ummms."

157. Leave something about your business.

As a beginning speaker you will be offered a free dinner and a hotel room if you have to stay overnight. But not money. For "payment" ask permission to leave something about your business on each seat or in each package of material they may hand out before your presentation. This can be a "get acquainted" gift certificate to have someone visit your place of business. Or the opportunity to leave your calling card and a description of your company.

158. Send a thank-you.

Write the person who contacted you to speak and thank them for giving you the opportunity. Mail this as soon as you return to your office.

159. Don't be afraid to be afraid.

If everyone else is, why should you be different? The biggest defense you have against fear is . . . Preparation, preparation, preparation (see Rule #1)

160. If you really want to speak . . . speak!

A young man once approached George Bernard Shaw and said he wanted to be a writer and what was Shaw's advice. Said Shaw, "Write."

Famed speaker Ken McFarland said the same thing to Bill Gove. Gove approached him after hearing the spellbinder captivate an audience. Gove asked, "I want to do what you do more than anything else in the world. How do I start?" And McFarland said, "Speak."

I once worried about doing a "bad" show and my wife Ruth said, "You'll never do a BAD show. You do so much work ahead of time and learn so much about the industry you can't have a BAD show. Yes, some shows will be better than others. And there are those magic moments when the world seems to stand still and the ovations are standing but they're rare. The rest were at least . . . good. And they were good because you prepared."

As usual, she was right.

8

THE 20 RULES OF PROMOTION

More than 4,000 came to our store to see Clarabell the Clown (a popular children's TV personality from the 50's and 60's).

That was topped by the 7,000 who came to see Mickey Mouse.

Each promotion we ran for our business was a single event that resulted in wide recognition in our community.

Promotions can be as large as these or as small as an annual sale.

There are certain steps that seem to work when planning your promotion. Here are 20 guidelines to follow.

161. Come up with the idea.

This is easier than it sounds. Ideas are all around you. If you doubt this, put together a brainstorming session with your staff. Sit down and talk about an upcoming holiday sale, event and ask, "How do we promote this?"

Someone in the group writes down all the ideas. No one is permitted to be negative. You'll be surprised at the great ideas you can elicit from your staff.

162. Make it unique.

For example:

Running a Grits Festival is unique. Grits is ground corn meal and a southern breakfast staple. A Piggly Wiggly supermarket manager in St. George, South Carolina, the heart of the "grits belt," saw they sold more grits per capita than the national average – four pounds vs one pound. Hey! – Why not have an annual "Grits Festival"? They have a Grits Eating Contest, floats, bands and the highlight is picking "Miss Grits." She is chosen by being weighed and then rolling in a tub of grits for a few minutes. She is then weighed again. Person with the most grits sticking to her body—wins.

Laugh if you will — but the small town of 2,500 now has 50,000 folks visiting every year for the annual Grits Festival.

163. Ask customers what they think of the idea.

An idea that sounds good in conversation or a winner on paper may often simply be not interesting to the consumer.

164. Make an outline of what has to be done.

List everything from all the advertising to who buys the balloons to who makes the phone call to who's in charge of exterior and interior displays to who's supervising the copy, art, handling the printing. Your outline will soon cover several pages.

165. Make a check list.
The outline of what has to be done is further broken down into specific tasks to be done by specific individuals.

166. Delegate authority.
Who does what. This can start out on a volunteer basis ("OK, who wants to find out the cost for silk screening 50 posters?") to simply assigning jobs. What you're REALLY doing: Involving everyone in the process.

167. Keep everyone in your business informed.
The #1 desire of people working in your business is "A feeling of being in on things." When someone is in charge of something it becomes THEIR project rather than the project of your business. And since they are coming back on a weekly basis to report progress, their pressure to accomplish is self-imposed.

Next: Tell your customers **first**. Before you advertise in the regular media. Mail them an advance notice of what's happening when.

168. Have a timetable.
What has to be done by when. This way each person is working on a specific deadline.

169. Have weekly meetings.
And when you are a couple of weeks away from the event, have daily meetings. Meetings are good not only because they provide a structure but also

because they give you the opportunity to exchange
ideas and solicit help from others in the group
working on other projects. If someone is unable to
make the contacts or find the information they need,
someone else will know another way to approach
the problem.

170. Weekly press releases.
To the newspaper, the radio, the TV station. Think of
a different "news" lead for each release. The
opening paragraph must be different but that-
which-follows can be a repeat of basic information.

171. Line up speeches at civic clubs.
The local Rotary, Kiwanis, Exchange, Elks, Moose
and other civic groups are always looking for a 20-
minute guest speaker at their weekly lunches. Call
them all. Volunteer to come and speak about your
upcoming event and the behind-the-scenes story on
what goes into this kind of promotion to make it all
happen.

172. Share your promotion with other businesses in your town.
You've come up with the idea, the details, the
planning. Why not invite noncompetitive businesses
to share in the fun. (And also share in the expenses.)
You mention their store in all the advertising done
for the promotion. This accomplishes two basic
purposes: Cuts down your costs. Makes the
promotion "bigger" because there are more
businesses involved.

173. FREE!

See what you can do with the most powerful word in the English language. Sure, the promotion is the big draw but what *else* are you doing to make the customer want to come? Some might not know or even be interested in the sports celebrity but will come if there is some special item at some special price. Or, better yet, give something away . . . FREE!

174. Run a sweepstakes.

Running a sweepstakes or giving a premium will automatically increase response. That's a good enough reason for you to add either one for your promotion. When we gave away a free trip for two to New Orleans or Disneyland during a promotion, our traffic increased ten percent! Work with other businesses to promote what they have to sell by bartering. "You give me the trip, I give you the advertising."

175. Testimonials.

This is an excellent time to have quotes from your customers on why they enjoy coming to your business. We had a salesman from the local radio station on hand to interview people on why they enjoyed shopping with us.

Picture the scene. It's celebrity time. Or it's special event time. The business is packed and everyone is having a great time.

Nine out of ten will give positive statements on why they came. Think about it: If you speak to people who just bought a specific brand car, they

107

will tell you all the reasons that car is best. If they did not, they would be saying they had poor judgment. A promotion is an excellent time to line up testimonials about you and your business.

176. Keep the promotion to a very specific time.

The narrower the better. One of our most famous promotional failures was our Irish Fortnight Event. We copied the idea from Neiman Marcus who was tremendously successful with this idea. But they were a huge department store, we were a small specialty shop. Two weeks for a promotion for them was fine. For us it was a near disaster. If we had held it for one day — or perhaps a two-day weekend, fine. But the longer the time period, the less excitement and desire to be there.

Our celebrities arrive and leave within a few hours. Our annual New Year's Day sale *which increased in volume every year for 25 consecutive years* started as a four-hour sale and was MORE successful than a three-day sale. The drama was intensified, the crowds lined up were longer, the purchases were faster and larger.

177. Have one last meeting with your staff just before the event.

It can be the night before or the morning of. Recheck who's responsible for what. By now the adrenaline will be almost uncontrollably gushing through everyone's veins and they will be hyped up and ready to go!

178. Added Value.

Add one more UNANNOUNCED event at the last moment. Entrepreneur Bill Veeck believed in this philosophy strongly. He would attract you to his ballpark with many announced specials and happenings. But somewhere, sometime during the game something "extra" happened — someone popped out of a cake in the middle of the field.

Or . . . "Lift up your seat to see if you have the lucky number for a free drink." We call this Added Value — the unexpected, unadvertised, unasked for . . . extra!

179. Include something to bring the customer back.

Mail order companies call this a "bounceback." You order something in the mail, they send it to you and include another offer for you to buy something again! My wife bought something from Spiegel, they sent the order and included a $20 gift certificate for her *next* purchase. She went though the catalogue, couldn't find anything she really wanted but bought a pair of jeans anyway. Didn't want to lose the $20.

And so: when all those folks arrive at your business for the promotion, make sure they have something in their hands to bring them back again.

Supermarkets do this by having NEXT week's specials tucked into the grocery bags as your purchases are packed.

180. Review.

No more than one week after the promotion is over, all the participants sit down and have a brainstorming session along the lines of "If we had to do it over again tomorrow what would we do differently?"

9

WHY DO THEY SAY "CLOSE" WHEN IT'S REALLY THE BEGINNING?

Talk to any teacher of selling and they remind you "All the time you are selling you have to remember your ABC's."

Really, what's that?

"Shorthand for *Always Be Closing*. No amount of training will make you successful if you don't know how to close a sale."

We'd be the first to agree that the objective of selling is to get the order. But why does it have to be..."the close."

The first definition of closing in Webster's says "to bar passage."

The second definition says "to deny access to."

The third definition: "to suspend or stop operations."

Fourth definition: "to bring to an end or period."

Doesn't make sense. Making the sale should be the beginning - not the end. What you are looking for: the lifetime value of the customer.

Can't do that if we close the door and walk away after making the sale.

I ask businesspeople, 'Do you know your 10 most important customers?' And CEOs or managers look strangely at me. If you don't know your best customers, you can't respond to them—or even thank them for being such an important customer.

This is*Customerization!*

Why this attention to the customers you have?

Because they are expensive to replace.

"I can't think of another investment which returns so high a yield," said Stanley Marcus, chairman of Neiman Marcus. "The increase in customer retention isn't something you buy, it's something you achieve."

Consider using focus groups. Every so often bring a group of your customers together and ask them what they DON'T like about your business. Don't ask what they DO like about your business. All that does is satisfy your own ego. Doesn't help, encourage or extend your business growth. Have someone take notes. Follow through with each suggestion. Write the person who came up with any idea and tell them what you did.

The more involved the customer becomes with you and your business, the more they not only remain a steady customer but also recruit other customers as well.

Same philosophy works with the Suggestion Box, the Telephone Hot Line. The more ways you give the customer a chance to become involved with your business, the more you learn about problems you might not otherwise have seen. Few businesses realize the importance of the customer who complains. They are giving you directions to follow.

Ted Levitt, head of marketing at Harvard Business School, likens this relationship to a marriage. He says, "The sale merely consummates the courtship at which point the marriage begins. How good the marriage is depends on how well the seller manages the relationship."

Will there be continued business? Added business? Troubles? Divorce?

Many times you will find your personnel trying to "protect the business." To make sure "the customer doesn't take advantage of you."

I once knew a credit manager who reported to the CEO and told him that because of his strict credit practices the firm suffered no losses the previous year.

"Really?" said the CEO, "you're fired."

What was he saying: "If you're that strict with all our customers, you're choking off new and future business. You're scaring the customer to look elsewhere."

It is no longer enough to make the sale. It's important, but not enough.

It is no longer enough to follow through. It's important, but not enough.

It is no longer enough to remind the customer you're still doing business in the same stand with new, improved merchandise. It's important, but not enough.

It is no longer enough to sell the product and the values that surround the purchase. It's important, but not enough

It's all of these — and more.

It's knowing about your customers' needs and desires and caring about them.

Some businesses are listening to their customers:

General Electric operates an 800 Answer Line. Call them 24 hours a day with any question about any GE product. They're waiting for your question with an answer.

General Mills has Betty Crocker's advisory service performing a similar benefit.

Proctor & Gamble has its own consumer hot line.

Gillette has a "vice president of business relations". The job: to check with people that buy Gillette to make sure they are happy and to solve any problems.

Supermarkets across the country have established special toll free lines to call for information on how to prepare meat, seafood, poultry — anything for dinner that evening *whether or not you bought the product in their store.*

Many salespeople feel after they make the sale they're off to greener fields and let someone else — anyone else — do the follow through. "That's not my job," they say. And they are wrong.

For the customer of tomorrow is their customer of yesterday. Salespeople must check to see if what-was-promised was performed. Otherwise the salesperson has to rebuild the relationship. Start all over again.

In the past, when the sale was made, it was, literally "closed."

That's why I have had, over the years, three different insurance salesmen. Each one came to me with the similar gambit of "Let us do an audit of the insurance you have and the premiums you are paying to see if you have the proper coverage."

O.K., fine. Each found better coverage at lower prices.

Each did a thorough and concise job.

Each persuaded me to switch from my present agent to them.

And each stopped calling me from the time the sale was made.

(Well, I do receive an annual birthday card from my present insurance agent with a stamped signature.)

Amazing! It's like the old burlesque joke where Tom approaches Sam and asks for a loan of ten dollars. Sam turns him down.

Tom, indignant, says, "How can you not give me the money? Wasn't I the person that drove you home from work all last week. Wasn't I the one who helped your daughter get into the college of her choice? Wasn't I the one that took care of your dog when you were on vacation?"

Sam thought about that for a moment and said, "That's all true. But what have you done for me lately?"

Will the relationship you have with your customer appreciate . . . or depreciate?

The answer is, simply, it's up to you.

You must reward your customer and become a partner with your supplier.

If you do both, with the ultimate goal of satisfying your customer, you will succeed in your business.

It's called: ***Customerization.***

Other products available from Raphel Publishing . . .

Tough Selling For Tough Times by Murray and Neil Raphel $ 19.95
Our latest book! Includes characteristics of successful business people.
Cassette companion to **Tough Selling for Tough Times** $ 9.95

the do-it-yourself direct mail handbook
by Murray Raphel and Ken Erdman $ 19.95
Totally revised 1992 edition. Everything you need to know to start
producing direct mail for your business.

Mind Your Own Business by Murray Raphel $ 19.95
Promotions that work in business. Lots of stories and ideas in this book.

Mind Your Own Business audio cassettes featuring Murray Raphel $ 39.95
Four audios with direct marketing success stories.

How to Find, Capture and Keep Customers by Stan Golomb $ 19.95
Proven promotions for small business owners.

Crowning The Customer by Feargal Quinn $ 19.95
Customer service tips from a leading Irish supermarket chain owner.

100 Ways to Prosper in Today's Economy by Barry Schimel, C.P.A. $12.95
Practical & proven strategies to improve your business' bottom line.

The Great Brain Robbery by Murray Raphel and Ray Considine $19.95
Steal marketing ideas that work.

Stealing The Competition video featuring Murray Raphel $ 39.95
How and why direct mail meets all your advertising needs.

Tooting Your Own Horn video featuring Murray Raphel $ 70.00
Murray's live presentation at the '92 FMI convention
telling supermarket ideas that work.
Video and workbook. $ 80.00

3 ways to order

Mail: Raphel Publishing
             12 S. Virginia Avenue
             Atlantic City, NJ 08401 U.S.A.
Phone: (609) 348-6646
Fax: (609) 347-2455

Check, American Express, Visa, MasterCard accepted
Add $3.50 for first item and $1.00 each additional item for shipping